You Tell Me

You Tell Me

He that hath ears to hear, let him hear.
- Matthew 11:15.

Roger Bell

Black Moss Press
2009

Library and Archives Canada Cataloguing in Publication

Bell, Roger, 1949-
  You tell me / Roger Bell.

Poems.
ISBN 978-0-88753-454-6

  I. Title.

PS8553.E4564 Y68 2009   C811'.54   C2009-901326-6

Cover Photograph by Marty Gervais

Published by Black Moss Press at 2450 Byng Road, Windsor, Ontario,
N8W 3E8. Canada. Black Moss books are distributed in Canada and
the U.S. by LitDistCo. All orders should be directed there.

Black Moss would like to acknowledge the Canada Council for the
Arts for its publishing program. Assistance was also provided by The
Ontario Arts Council this year.

ONTARIO ARTS COUNCIL
CONSEIL DES ARTS DE L'ONTARIO

Le Conseil des Arts | The Canada Council
du Canada | for the Arts

PRINTED IN CANADA

I dedicate this book to Val, with whom I celebrated 35 married years in 2008. She lets me be.

I would like to thank all of those people both brave and trusting enough to give me their stories. Without their openness, this book would not exist: Jeannette Aster, Jacob Bachinger, Scott Black, Betty Carter, Anne Connell, Marty Gervais, John Hartman, Ed Hunt, George Lee (in memoriam), John Lee, Andrew MacMenemy, John Philips, She whose husband was away on business, Joe Sherman (in memoriam), Betsy Struthers, John Tyndall.

I wish to express my appreciation to the editing team at Black Moss Press: Chris Andrechek, Jasmine Ball, Jessie Beatty, Braydon Beaulieu, Christina Coletti, Kimberly Daigneau, Kate Fathers, Alex Gayowsky, Vanessa Kaiser, Snijana Leitao, Donna Luangmany, Serein Makkawi, Lauren McDonald, Stephanie Mihajlovic, Rachel Olsen, Karl Parakenings and Amber Pinsonneault. The eighteen of them poured their sweat and blood into this project. They challenged me, they gave me fresh eyes. Because of them this is a much better book.

I must also gratefully acknowledge the aid of two friends and fellow poets: Betsy Struthers, who is not afraid to pare and praise in the same breath, suggested long-lining some of these poems and futher cast her honest eye on several of these pieces to tighten them; and John Lee, who, as he has faithfully done over our 33 years as buddies, keeps helping me hone.

"Jeannette's tale" was published in *Bonjour Burgundy* (Mosaic Press)
"Just a bit of small talk" first appeared in *Six Voices* (Hidden Brook Press)

Table of contents

Tonight she's going dancing

She feels gut kicked
and breath bereft
she feels maybe she
should just quit

but instead tonight she'll go out dancing
put on her electric blue wig for practice
put on a strapless satin evening gown
to hell with being bone-weary
and breastless
put on a piss and vinegar smile
kick up her heels
and howl at heaven

though the bartender shake up chemo cocktails
with a blue-veined translucent hand
though the strobes pulse white and nuclear
like crazed doves about Chernobyl
though the band play *Nearer, My God, To Thee*
and the dance floor tilt while the ship goes down
though tomorrow and tomorrow and tomorrow and tomorrow
be remorseless and cold, and the lifeboats leaky
and the water morbid and murky and dark

she'll dervish dance with a man called Death
she'll swing him round 'til the sky stands still
with their lips locked and their wild eyes fused
until one or both can't stand the pace

only then will she acquiesce to morning.

The speed of being

Before he was a biker, he was just a boy
who held her hand carefully as they
aimlessly circumnavigated the unstated
and explored the railway line, laughing
and kicking clinkers into the thickets
intoxicated by a resonance of sweet peas
that sprawled unexpurgated along the embankments.
Occasionally they stopped, awkward
at the dictates of convention, *boyfriend, girlfriend*
exchanged clumsy kisses, their novice mouths
unsure of protocol, their tongues
firmly held behind closed teeth
their fingers splayed and unsure on
the hard, strange rib-bones of the other.

At the season's last bonfire, with school
and distance around the curve of Labour Day
they exchanged a long shadow-sheltered clinch
amazed at the hammering of their hearts –
time-pieces urgent with gears and turnings –
but the searching catcalls of friends, the seeking light
drowned out their sounds of wonderment
and their lips barely lingered before
he was gone
and she hardly thought of him
over those long and windowless months of drifted winter.

So she was jolted from her next abstraction in
the blustery yearnings of Wuthering Heights

when, the first feral afternoon of July
preceded by thunder
and the raised heads of nearby cattle
he purred his big black Harley
onto the prim front lawn of her cottage
said simply, *Let's ride.*

His hair was much longer
curled about his collar
but it would be all right
she nodded, mounted
and he brought his heel down
hard
to kick the motor to life
and flicked the throttle.

He took her out into the hills back beyond the town
where the road's dips and curves hide what's coming.
She leaned, let the fullness of summer wash over her
as they wound along dazed roads
           in the drugged heat of Sunday rolling
           and she felt the speed of being
           and she felt the thrum of knowing
           where her bare legs squeezed the saddle
           around his blue-jeaned buttocks
           and boy and girl and Harley
           were unified and holy.

She wrapped her arms around him, holding
on, laid her head against him, saw
for the first time, the tattoo

a naked snake woman, twisting
crawling up the blue ridge of his spine
and she smelled something brutish
in the leather of his jacket
and she trembled with a different heart's thud
her young breasts aching into his back

and when he slowed
and swung the bike down a gravel path
into a secluded clearing
above a dry creek bed
and cut the motor
the silence was so sudden

        she wanted movement and blur
        she wanted nothing to hold her

but
then
he was pressing her into the sand
with his insistence, and she knew
they had come to a hard place
past grazing kisses and linked fingers
far from friendship.
He was such a weight on her
his hands bruising where they tore at her blouse
his knee digging into the desperate ramparts of her thighs
his breath stinking of self, tobacco and want.

She fought him in silence, they
wrestled, rolled she scratched his
face, he hit her, she
bit him, hissed
I'll tell your mother!

The day drained
and he stood, his eyes hooded.
He started the bike
she started to breathe
got on behind him but could not
touch him
not once on the straight road home.

Everywhere

She swears she sees him everywhere.

Sometimes in the barn echoing with the faint complaints of sheep
long ago banished like sinners, maintaining until the very moment
the tailgate slammed shut, their innocence, their hurt, their need to
stay here where they were born. He will pass in an aura of dust motes
between her and wind-whipped windows where winter sun slants into
the stable, she'll see him with his arms outspread, herding the reluctant
toward food and rest, she'll hear his voice low and insistent. Calming.

Sometimes in the kitchen as she putters at the stove, her back turned
to the table set still for both, the eggs poaching sedately and the
bread beginning to brown in the toaster. She will hear him cough
and turn the pages of the paper, she'll hear him between stories rest,
pick up his cup and sip the hot tea, hear him unscrew the cap of a
sealer and carefully spoon three preserved peach halves into a saucer,
meticulously cut them up with a spoon pressed between calloused
thumb and forefinger, and slowly savour each piece, as if summer can
indeed be kept by sugar and hard work.

Sometimes, of an evening, the slap shut of the screen door behind him.
He'll be there prying off his work-heavy boots, the day's chores finally
done, he'll shuffle to the sink and wash his hands, dry them on the tea
towel the way she's asked him not to do for forty years, leave it draped
cockeyed on the handle of the oven door.

Sometimes in the living room, sagged into the big chair, tilted back,
feet raised, a hole in the heel of the left worksock, his belt undone to
let supper settle. He flicks on the mindless box and disappears a while

far from the fickleness of crops into some game show or cop drama, the screen a bit fuzzy since that storm last fall skewed the antenna. She has asked him to fix it but he hasn't found the time. Later on her way to bed she'll find him, heavy with sleep, his chin on his chest, his fingers interlaced across his proud belly.

Sometimes she will not trust herself, a widow awakening in the wall-creaking wind that tumbles through the tall black spruce, afraid the weight of the star-laden night will crush her house upon the hill, but then she'll feel him roll over behind her, spoon against her, his right arm a reassurance flung across her ribs, his breath a balm upon her neck, his big heart a familiar syllable that lulls her back into better dreams.

Immaculate, a deception

She was a Daughter of the Blessed Virgin, so unbesmirched by the filth and dross of ordinary living that when she went to confession she had to invent sins to satisfy the restless priest behind the expectant screen of the booth. *I pinched my brother just to hear him squeal. I took my father's daily paper and wrinkled it before he got home from work to do the crossword. I did not kneel before bed last night and so I dreamt of the Devil.* She was so good the sun broke through the saddest clouds to crown her in glory, so good that willow trees knelt to her passing and the breeze that lifted her was streaked with frankincense and myrrh.

She was adored, and trusted, so when she asked to attend the Catholic Youth dance, why, of course she could, of course goodness and mercy would follow her all the days and nights of her life.

It was the slow dance that began it, it always is. The priests and nuns, stiff in the corners, had osprey eyes, but despite them the boy pressed into her, and some consequence began to thicken in her abdomen, some spring swelled in her breast, and when he walked her home in the humid night, his hand enclosing hers, the darkness seemed to deepen, the cicadas began to gossip. And on the seeming safety of her porch, without warning, he slid his arms around her waist and pulled her to his heat and crushed her mouth with his, slid his tongue, like some lovely serpent, along her teeth and voice, her knees melting along with her purity, but the strong boy held her from tumbling. Then he was gone.

She did not sleep at all that long night of reckoning, she tried praying to what was just a cracked ceiling, she feared she was now pregnant, spoiled like butter left in the sun. She rose early, went to First Mass, but avoided Confession, she knew she could not breathe in there, with something bigger than a lie choking her; when she genuflected for Communion the light ran blood red through the stained glass windows, the Blessed Virgin stared down at her with hard marble eyes. When the priest flicked the wafer toward her open mouth, she saw razor-missed stubble on his chin, imagined his thick tongue entering her like an impeachment, and before the Body of Christ could burn into her flesh she fainted at his feet, fruit fallen hard from the nurture of the One True Tree.

Tumbler

She tells me her husband is away on business.
I can think of no good reason for her candour
and it settles on me like the fast-falling snow
when I leave the store heavy with groceries.

My husband is away on business, until Thursday.
Why so specific? I think about her eyes, green and frank
instead of, as I should, about the wet, insistent snow
that my wipers cannot clear, that my wheels cannot handle
so that the car veers toward the ditch's drop-off
and when I correct, I over-correct and slide helplessly
into the oncoming lanes of snow-ghosted traffic
and barely miss the eager wedge nose of a plow.

I arrive home shaken, the near-death adrenaline coursing
an ugly mix of fear, desire, fear, and I think of her, alone
the light waning, the drifts gathering wantonly about her house
and she in the kitchen, in the darkness, in the snowbound warmth

her small hands curled comfortably around a tumbler of scotch
and on the back of her tongue, that tongue that set me thinking
the fire of invitation, she, by the window in her husbandless kitchen
barely moving, barely breathing, waiting, watching, waiting.

Jeannette's tale

With all this beneficence I do not know
how to accommodate what Jeannette is telling
because in the telling much blood is spilled.

With the evening sun's balm upon us
and on the lawn, the long table laden
with local wine and a profusion of food
with the melting light buttering the valley descending
descending away from us
toward Vitteaux and the eight Charolais
creamy patches of meadow dreamily
grazing their way upward to where they will arrive
like promises in the ritual of dusk

here at La Roche d'Hys, in the heights of Bourgogne
where the escarpment spills its guts
down, and down further
like a confessor who never tires of telling

here where three springs meet in a Y
like a dowser's rod, like a pelvis and thighs
promising where they join

below that ancient listening wall
the Pagans gathered, and on the Rock
La Roche d'Hys, the slab of offering
they sacrificed those so lovingly chosen
split their chests in the inverted Y
the way the coroner or the augur does

so the last heartthrobs of the pure pounded
into the cooling air and shimmered there
dying songs, spent voices, descending
into all this proffered verdancy.

And just there, toward Dijon
the highest hill, called *La Justice*
is now a field of grain, a golden filler of fat bellies
but three centuries ago the townspeople mobbed
and trundled the condemned in taunted carts up
and up to die on gallows
constructed of strong wood and no mercy.
When the braided rope went taut
and all the breaths of all the gathered
snapped in their chests like bowstrings
their eager gazes arrowed up
to where the strangling one dangled and kicked
at the inefficient air, eyes beginning to bulge
around that last long darkening look
at a world going downhill down
down the hill and into death.

There, past the farthest fence, where the Vitteaux Road
bisects the valley lengthwise
the Germans tramping north to fortify Paris
prodded with gun barrels the mayor
of Grosbois and others rudely gathered
pushed them to mass slaughter
past cattle who know that sullen feel. But
the brave farmer of La Roche d'Hys
felled many trees to block their progress

so that angry like green-jacketed bees
the soldiers swarmed up the hill to the shaded yard
and ordered all the food and water
but Antonin Mias spat
Jamais de la vie!
Over my dead body!
and they complied, cut him down in a burst
and in the same hail of hatred
his neighbour, François Jacob.
The two dropped face down
never to rise and taunt again
though their felled forest frustrated still.
And then in spite, in a frenzy of fire
the Germans torched everything
the house, the sheds, the barn
which burned long into the starry night
of their vexation.

Soon after dawn, the Resistance shoved two German soldiers
into the stony glare of Mme la veuve Mias
asked her her pleasure, and she shot back
Deux pour deux, tuez les, tuez les!
An eye for an eye, kill them, kill them!
turned quickly from the pleading looks
of the blond young men who no more had time
to consider their days declining
than revenge bored bluntly through them
and they tumbled like roof beams
beside the still smoldering barn
and there lie buried still, today, long after.

Long after, and here we are gathered
in a place so tranquil, oh so gentle
when we raise our brimming glasses
to toast the confluence of our beings
here where three springs meet and meld
here where the valley opens
an eye full of longing, the sun
re-emerges from behind invading clouds
to crown *La Justice* in glory
and to embellish
this wine of our communion and
the crusty bread broken and
scattered upon the long table
and those eight Charolais
who graze placidly and wait for darkness
to disappear like whispers
of the long gone dead.

Andrew MacMenemy

The big boats rumbled in last night
to the tranquil little bay on Beausoleil
and cranked wide their stereos
their generators voodooing gasoline
into heavy metal fumes, seared meat
beer bottles breaking, and sleeplessness.

This morning in his kayak
he glides among their hung-over shadows
hears the now muted thrum of thermogenesis
as if these craft are all comatose
and these machines, these eclipsed suns, are
their life support, their beat and breath.

He imagines himself a sacred euthanizer
paddle dipping through their drugged dream
deftly slipping aboard each yacht and with his gentle hands
extinguishing their fossil-fuelled hearts

so that true sound melts back in like first light above the eastern shore
and the loons, long bullied into silence, revive, and praise him
with the rippling of their joy.

Inverted world

Run, do not think, I do as I sinew along paths among redwoods that support the faint distant sky on this barely born Pacific day, still more night than morning. Run, do not think, I do, my feet silently indenting eons of soft shedding and dying, my body a smooth machine inhaling/exhaling all with little wonder to where again it is absorbed and expelled, my passage barely noticed.

Run, do not think, I think I see movement in the dense underbrush above, a begrudging of ferns, a slight shimmer of seedlings, a bird spooked and whirring, tilted by fear so I stutterstep, realize just where I am, the word *cougar* slinking from behind widening eyes, my throat constricting, my heart hammering blood too close to my skin. I turn, sprint back the way I hope I came, trust the reverse of each Y that brought me here, wherever I am in this dense puzzle of lush hills, the back of my neck sweating and glowing, they attack from above and behind, this I know, as I run into a man-made clearing where buildings rise and pavement hardens beneath my feet, and walkers and talkers greet me as if they have always known me, though I feel a stranger in this strange and feral land.

I pant the question, *Are there big cats in there?* point to the shadows grown darker with sunstrength. *Oh, yes,* they seem awed, *you didn't go in there alone?* And the weight of that last word on my heart.

Ron comes in now with his story of a friend and his wife who heedlessly hiked the hills of California until two other hikers, easterners, were mauled; the man was killed, they never did find all of him to bury, the woman left clinging to the rearranged tendon and skin that her life had become. Ron's friends bought chain mail to wear as a veil of immunity against those merciless teeth. And locals told them too, *Wear a mask on the back of the head to confuse the cat. Become two-faced, they don't know where to attack.* They scoured the town but all they could find was Richard Nixon's leering visage, so ironic, they despised him for Viet Nam, Cambodia, Watergate, the disrespect he brought upon the Stars and Stripes, but fear and practicality won out and they wore Tricky Dicky, he looked back for them, like the tail gunner in a B52, low over Hanoi.

It becomes a kind of feeding frenzy, someone else kicks in with the story of someone who knew someone who wore a bicycle helmet into cat country, one with a mirror on it. He looked always backwards, tremulously into that inverted world, until vertigo tracked him down, he began to falter, which is which became which is which twisted 180 degrees and when he spun around to reorient, ahead became back, his compass danced so wildly he blacked out. Came to, half an hour later, face pressed into the giving ground, and saw beside him in the soft earth, big paw prints where a cougar had hesitated, studied him, and finding him wanting, padded off. Rumour is he has never been the same, never found the true direction.

And now today, on the other side of the continent, to finish this, Betty tells me of Mexico, of walking the arid west end of Copper canyon, and being told by her native guide that centuries ago they warred with neighbours and the heads of the dead enemy were reverentially removed, the skulls bisected and carved hollow like gourds, then smoked dry and worn when needs be, yin/yang on the head, front/ back, me/my foe, into the parched hills where the big cats ranged, death protecting from death.

I think, we are so vulnerable, the neck so exposed: spine brain jaw tendons muscles carotid jugular. No eyes in the back of our head, we are not meant to enter these fierce heavens, the hills and the woods of the puma, we are meant only to look forward into a world de-forested, a tangle of pavement, heat, steel, we are meant to wander broad broken sunburnt sidewalks, the sky above obscured by a yellow soup of ozone and exhaustion, around us the rant of pile-drivers, jackhammers and curses, we are meant to squint straight down that long pitiless expressway to the death of the soul. We are meant to see it coming.

What his brother saw

When he dared to stare into the small
hard
pupil
of the BB gun
what his brother saw
was
a concept more meagre
than a seed.

What his brother saw
as he squeezed the trigger
was the seemingly stupid world
grow ironic faster than laughter
blossom into a vision
as white and complete
as a purview of suns
swaying on dying stems.

The days of our lives

Herb's mother recorded the minutiae of the long-unfolding days:
the sun-bleached mornings of sheets dancing on lines
the dust-mote moments that floated
across the carpeted afternoons of Newton-Robinson
the drift-white featureless evenings
when winter closed them in
and roads became less than murmurs
in the dimmed-down conversation of winds.

She wrote in pen, and when that failed
pencil with a worn-flat eraser, an HB that she
sharpened with a paring knife
the same one she used to skin Spy apples for the pies
that won the prize each year at Stayner Fall Fair.
She wrote in hard-bound books and scribblers with names like Hilroy
that she remembered using as a child in the one-roomed school
where sunlight and the waft of fresh-mown hay
made her dream of life far beyond these hills.
She wrote as if God Himself had commissioned her
to paint each page a Sistine ceiling with her words
as if missing even a day for the ague or the curse
or the squalling of a teething child would be dereliction
a sin of omission, a gap in the growing bones of the world.

So when she died, she left this legacy, and Herb and Anne
sat flummoxed among boxes of daily diaries
leaf upon leaf, both stapled and glued
day after week after month after year, dated carefully
and arranged chronologically down the passage of her time.

They began to aimlessly wander the recondite corridors
of her chronicles, opening dusty doors, each room a museum
of the esoteric, preserved like last summer's string beans
in jars in the dim and dirt-floored cellar.
They shuffled and read but it proved so heavy they had trouble
breathing, began to hyperventilate, often racing past decades
trying to find something blinding, some venal sin, some outrage
some soul-destroying stain upon the page
something tawdry or bawdy, something like The Days of Our Lives
that might lift itself from the mundane like a hawk
above ground mist. Perhaps:
Your father is not your father or *After the affair ended he left*
on the midnight train or *I once contemplated suicide* or
What I saw I shouldn't tell but… or *We buried the stolen money*
beneath a full moon three paces past the gravestone of my aunt.
Something. But all they found and found again was nothing
the bric-a-brac, the ticking of the clock faithfully transcribed.

What does one do with a surfeit of polished stones?
What does one do with a million words as dull as chalk
upon the tongue? They could not do her the dishonor
of leaving them at the curb with the stained chair
or the festering jars of jam whose time had come and gone.
They could not burn them with the leaves that lay unraked
among the shrubs, or sell them at auction among
the chipped plates and saucerless cups. So they buried them
in her garden and her flower beds in a solemn ceremony
made sadder by a descent of cowbirds, interred them
marked only by the heel of the round-nosed shovel.
They buried them among the phlox and ox-eyed daisies and peonies
she tended as assiduously as she wrote. Now

when spring arrives from the last scraps of melting
and the sun climbs finally high enough to warm the good dark earth
the plants that push their way towards the welcome air
all have voices that sing like this:

*Today the Reverend and his lovely wife, she has the
tremors, poor thing, came by for tea. We talked of
next Sunday's hymns, and of how the organ needs repairing before
Christmas. I served cucumber sandwiches and gingersnaps. They
left at about four-thirty. At five it began to rain, and still is.*

*Today was grocery day. I piled the girls into my big old faithful
Buick and drove them to Bradford. After shopping we went to
lunch at the Chinese restaurant. I had, as always, the Combination
Plate #3. I found the pineapple chicken balls particularly succulent.
Tonight the wind is from the north. It promises change.*

*Today I cleaned the place thoroughly. It has been a long
winter. It always amazes me what accumulates behind and
underneath furniture. You have to pull things from their
regular places to get at it. It is exceptionally clear tonight,
fully lit by the moon. If you step outside and let your eyes
wander, you can see for miles.*

Outer darkness

He was different
and he knew it
that blue swoon that slid over him
every time he tried to converse
the tightness in his chest
like a sweater that would never fit
he decided not to try
instead he consigned himself
to outer darkness
rather liked onlyness
the sweet silence of solipsism
grew to savour himself

until the December he rented her spare room
and the night the prairie wind
hardened the sloughs
and drove the cattle into huddles
shook the shuttered windows
and turned his small cell so inhospitable
even by burrowing deep
he could no longer avoid it

he opened
his door
and saw by the glow from under
her door
that she was still awake
before his nerve could quaver
he slid paper

and its shaky supplication
I'm cold
into the shining chance
then waited in the shivering hall
his bare feet no longer content with limbo

then
there she was, open
he felt the heat of invitation
she led him to the bed
anointed him in light
gave him the name *Lover*
that brought him back from exile.

The blow-job funeral

i) The story arises

The story arises on a day bright
with the promise of an Arctic high
after a week morose with cloud.
The artist and I agree the death he describes
appeals so much more than

putting in a sun-roof
with a 12-gauge, Jackson Pollocking
the ceiling with your final affirmation

or flailing off the Jacques Cartier Bridge into
the grinding ice of the grey, grim St. Lawrence
to be pummeled and buffeted until you wash up
a broken, bloated discovery of children, near Rimouski

or laying your head on the tracks, feeling the comforting
kiss of the polished steel on your stubbled cheek
hearing the rush of the 4:30 homeward bound express
coming to crush the last light from your soul-sad eyes.

ii) I'll bet

I'll bet when the professor shook down his drawers
in a frenzy in the parking lot
of the golf course closed for the season
reclined in the heated leather seat

felt his student's young fire absorb him
her tongue start its practiced circumnavigation
he didn't want to die.
I'll bet she didn't expect to finish the affair
with a face full of dead cock.
But his heart was ready, it felt the sympathetic urge
to burst, and his cry of *Jesus!* which she
mistook for blessed release, was really a blade of pain
impaling him in his heaving
and may also have been his shocked recognition
of the tsk-tsking of his Saviour
peering in like some leery voyeur
through the Buick's breath-fogged windshield
past the rosary swinging from the skewed mirror..

I'll bet she didn't want her lips listed
as *cause of death* on some coroner's report.
I'll bet he didn't want to be memorialized
at what the snickering locals called *the blow-job funeral.*

But life isn't a board game, sometimes dying doesn't wait
for you to make a choice of time or place or instrument
Mrs. Peacock hanging herself in the study with the rope
her stiletto heels dancing vainly in the wan air
while books all around her go unread
sometimes death holds the bones
rattling them like ice cubes in a thin hand
sometimes you take whatever's thrown, whenever
lie back, relinquish, be grateful
that you die with a stiffy, balanced
on the knife-edge above orgasm

that you are pushed by desire
long before despondency whispers
long before you must jump.

iii) She / They / He

She
isn't there, of course
that would be too brightly bold
she's some distant elsewhere
nursing a clutched crystal tumbler
of amber grief, neat
gazing stolidly from a high window
into the blue shadow of a frozen stream.

They
are there, of course
decorum demands it
his wife dressed in a tasteful blend
of black and shame
sure everyone who envelops
her trembling hand in theirs
is delving the depths of what she lacks
that deep dark aquifer that drove
her husband to drink elsewhere
but her gaze holds steady
pushes back each accusation
his children safe
in the arms of ignorance
too young to comprehend

that Daddy died with his lust
like a fuchsia lipstick sunset
smeared across their horizon.

He
of course
looks oddly at peace
his wandering heart stilled
the dick that stopped it
now just a sleeping bird dog
wrapped in its own final dreams
beyond the hush of words
curled beside a warm wood stove
after a long and fruitful hunt.

iv) Artist, if you can

Artist, if you can, paint this:
layer a purple casket
onto a dais of gold leaf
against a pounding
blood-red background
all viewed reverentially from below
like the Ascension
like the Hindenburg
rising toward its destination.

From out of the polished box
grows a thick-stemmed white
mutated mushroom

the gilled glans pushing
toward the ebony vault of sky
to where she waits
her wings the humming silver orbits of electrons
her eyes a crystal tide of grief
her undraped thighs a white field of drifted wind
and her mouth an O
   a deep inviting O
a pink round well of a vowel
ready to take you in.

Surfeit

You tell me it began with a distancing of yourself from yourself
becoming your own enemy
with an arcing in your fingers' tips
the way they sizzled the first time
they shyly approached the impetuous skin
of a naked woman.

You tell me it began with surfeit
too much protein, too much message
antibodies in minnow frenzy churning the too small
pond of your flesh
swarming the myelin sheaths of your nerves, and nibbling
unable to differentiate bait from hook from line
until frayed wires sent mixed metaphors and the phone
kept ringing and the lights kept burning
in the unoccupied rooms of your brain.

You tell me your muscle memory has grown forgetful.
Stair risers are not what they seem
you must tread carefully
read like Braille the descending wall
so you do not walk out into space
like the hapless coyote who misses the roadrunner
runs out of solid ground
stands looking at us with woebegone eyes
realizes he has been paltered with
waves sadly before he plummets.

You tell me when you play catcher and try
to return the ball to the pitcher
the pitcher is what he seems
but not where he seems
and the seams on the white sphere
are like clumsy sutures on a Frankenstein skull, they mock you
as they wobble toward the wrong field of right field.
You extend your arm, hold out your hand
as far away as possible
regard it as one regards an unnamed object, warily
as if while you dreamed
anaesthetized by your sense of all that's fair
some malicious surgeon
little more than a girl de-limbing her Barbies
twisted off your extremities
and re-attached those of a cadaverous clone

or some drunken farmer grafted
a pear branch onto the trunk of a cherry tree
and from then on it's all been chears and perries
strange and tasteless fruit.

As you tell me it even affects your sex life
you stare at the extrinsic flesh
at those dumb digits, crook the index, uncrook it, say
Yep, the old pussy finger ain't what she used to be.

There is silence, both of us shocked at what you've revealed
followed by an amazed onrush of laughter, deep and lewd
as if we are once again those young men of forty years ago
who found lust in every energy, and celebrated its being.

We laugh, loud and proud and rueful. Of course we laugh
while the bright autumn day short-circuits
into a million pin-prick stars.
What the fuck else can we do?

Eclipse

Conversations over coffee have a way of ebbing.

When the speaker, spent, leans down her face into the balm of steam rising from the cup, bathes away winter's bathos in the aromatic rising mists of someplace far away, parts her lips to take of the chalice. When the listener drifts upon the stream of words like Odysseus mesmerized by Calypso's honeyed voice offering the soft white massage of immortality, the deathlessness of days beneath the aimless cloudless sky, nights beneath the full eye of the ministering moon. When musing turns them both in upon themselves, talking is replaced by reflective sipping, the heat upon the receptive tongue and down the eager throat, an involution.

She had first told me about the eclipse, about how the full moon would slowly stumble into the adumbration of the earth, and be numbed into nearly non-being, thence into a blush and a hiatus, like a breath held in anticipation of the Rapture, how it would then re-emerge and the shadows on the snow would stretch like cats awakening and deepen into substance.

We discussed the little boy who vanished in Tofino when his father turned his back and the child was swept by the cupidity of waves off into the unforgiving greyness, the tiny body tossed, probably never to be found, never held one last time, never buried with his toys, and we both wondered how the father could live after that, and even if he did, what a hollowed out wanderer he'd be, the decaying albatross of his culpability hanging so heavy around his neck that all he'd see were his tears wetting his blind and blundering feet, seeking any path at all but the one that led back and back to that pitiless shingle.

And I had told her about my nephew Trevor, taken at thirteen by a
whim of water barely two inches deep, but enough to suppress breath,
enough to still the blond boy's heart like a memory going cold in the
confines of a photograph in a dust-covered album on a shelf in the
spare room of our hearts.

And she then brought up Johnny, her red-haired brother who got
cancer at age five, eaten from the inside so that he became light enough
even his siblings carried him easily from the bedroom to the gazebo
her father built him in the yard, hoping the air of the garden would
transfuse him, that the leaves would teach him how to sing again in
that green child's voice so sweet the trees shiver at its passing, so pure
the birds rise as one and fly up after it enviously as it arrows toward
the heavens. But he failed, became more and more translucent, the
indecisions between breaths more pronounced, and eventually every
love shone right through him. She remembers, or thinks she does,
writing him a letter that they tucked in the pocket of his burial suit,
but she has no recollection of the words she used to wish him back,
she was only six, it's sixty years, and the fading is almost complete.
But she does remember her father, the Catholic so devout he'd have
been a priest had it not been for the allure of her mother's Presbyterian
smile, her father rampaging throughout the next few years, cursing
Holy Mother Church and the God who murdered children, his visage
scoured by grief, stinging like the slapped face of a spurned suitor.

Her mother simply took to her bed, dazed between sheets that did not
settle on her or settle her, a disquieted refugee who cannot find the way
home, though she knows the conflict is over. Her father did his best
but children need more than grief. Until one day the doctor told the
mother he'd seen enough, and physically lifted her from her misery,
told her she had other children still of this earth, and they needed

her and the shelter of her bosom, and that was that, she took again to the house and the chores, but she was never happy, and the food she cooked stuck to the pots and the clothes she ironed had wrinkles like old skin and the dust hid in corners where she could not find it, though her knees grew chafed from searching. And oh, that vacant place at the table where every evening a plate and cutlery were laid, but never used, oh the onus of that truant guest. The children that she later bore like afterthoughts never knew the brave her that had come along from Scotland with three babes, the woman who waited for her husband at war and kept the word *family* burning like a stove that wants to go cold. There was a gap in the looks she gave the latecoming children, always there was some tenderness reserved, as if she was keeping back the best fruit from her pies, as if the smiles she squeezed out were practiced in front of a cracked mirror on a cold morning. When she brushed their hair, it was someone else's hair. She lived to be decades older than she wished, far past the wreckage of her husband, and her eyes were always somewhere just beyond. The day she died her daughter lay beside her on the bed and watched the springs wind down, the lungs give in, until her last sigh, a long-held languishing, or a greeting for someone special arriving finally from across a vast need. *Johnny.*

There was an eclipse that night, but the sky could not make up its mind, I had to wait. For the veil of snow to part like a curtain on the stage where the moon was the sole performer. For the sly progress of diminuendo until the sphere became somber, then ruddy, as if kissed by Mars. Until a thin grin appeared across the bottom, and soon the prodigal laughed out across the land like a cocksure boy that was never really gone, just reclining in the welcome shade while time tipped further, now back, and so painfully bright, it brings tears.

I know a hill

I know a hill, she told him on their first date and
took him by the hand as if he were helpless, which
he was, having already drowned in her eyes and
her fervour. *I know a hill*, and on their rollerblades glided him blind

to where Mulcaster dips dangerously toward the bay
and before he could consider, she yanked him around
the corner and down dizzyingly toward the lights at Dunlop
the wind swallowing her yell to *time the intersection with the green*

which they did not do, he could see dying coming both ways red
they did not do, just slalomed and lucked in a tucked closed-eyed
scream between oncomings, found themselves on the next descent
and a sharp turn, the grin on her face so crystalline it nearly pained

and in the thrashing of his heart, he forgot her nickname was *Insane*
forgot his fear and held on hard to her, has kept on holding
down every hill that brought them this far.

Just a bit of small talk

George leans across the table
we are co-conspirators away from noise
and eaters in the middle of eggs and sausage and too much toast.
Just a little small talk
and he twice taps my wrist lightly
with forked index and middle fingers
as if dowsing for interest,
likes what he finds, and begins:

Fat cows are cheap cows.
See that silo?
those others down the way?
monuments
to pride
and poor planning
nobody keeps cattle
now.
Young guy took out a loan to build them
and it
broke 'im.
these last two words leaned on.
I gaze at the tall tombs he speaks of
they must echo inside,
hollow with irony
rank with foreclosure
and the aftersmell of silage.

A pause as Irene pours coffee, then:
Just a bit of small talk, Roger

two brothers down the road
trapped fox, muskrat, coon
made four to five thousand a year
nice bit o' pocket money
but Russia fell apart
looks east, as if at crumbling Kremlin
walls just beyond the yard
and those...... animal people....
last year those brothers shipped the same furs
and got, again, wrist tap, like a fluttering heart,
375 dollars.
They sold the traps, before it broke 'em.
Just a bit of small talk:
we raise soybeans now.
Wheat? Well, who can compete?
the state of Iowa grows thirty times
as much grain as all of Canada
single wrist rap, more urgent now
and the wool we shipped last
didn't bring enough
to hardly pay for the gas
to take it to market.

This isn't small talk, George
it's the earth tapping out its warning
on our pulse points.

The dishes cleared, we walk outside
into the hazy filter of October
around where the black barns
sag in a slow sensual dance of wind and time.

The paint is like old skin
and I don't suppose anyone
will ever paint again
where the mows bulge against the bowed ribs.
An old dog with a flecked face
rests in the corner
of the doorway by a whitewashed wall.
She's an Australian sheep dog
like her former owner –
retarded
strides past his own joke
traded a Suffolk ewe for her mother
though I'll admit, she sure can cut
a sheep from a flock.
A calico cat chews on the dog's ear;
the dog ignores this;
the sun soaks away all abuse.

Lookit these Lincolns,
best probably in the world
isn't a flock in North America
doesn't have our breeding in them
and this isn't hubris which speaks
it's the soil, the soul
those ewes (he says it *yows*)
see the way they stand?
leg on every corner
good bones
good heads
and this ram
Johnny, hold his head

and his son slips out of his poet's clothes
the man I know becomes the boy
his father knew at Glencoe Fair
expertly grabs the skittish sheep
like a faith healer feeling
the shaggy head for pain
and in an instant
the beast snorts once and breathes easy.
Stick your face in here, boys
and smell this wool.
George parts the heavy fleece
and I find my face deep
deep in a world where I've never been.
These sheep clip twenty five pounds
others just six
and his face breaks open
grinning,
feel the lanolin, I do
George has me now
and the stuff rubs into my hands like long love.
Grandpa lay dying in bed,
November to March
in his woolen underwear and socks.
Emily bathed him for the wake
she was a nurse, you know
said he was soft as a baby
she'd never seen a cleaner body.
Never wear nylon, boys.
Grandpa was a strong Liberal.
If a yellow dog was running for the Grits
he'd vote for 'im.

He once told me
a Tory looks like a Liberal
who's had a good dose of salts.

And back into the barn we go
past a sign warning CROSS RAM!
I fear, for I have no desire
to feel myself pinned
between these stone walls
and the unyielding thickness of a ram's skull
full only of fighting, food and copulation.
We see the bucks with bellies painted different colours
and covered ewes
like Hester Prynnes of the farm
their backs badged blue or red or yellow.
And then George swings outside as the tour quickens:
That cement trough there
was built seventy-five years ago
see where the horses and cattle have
rubbed with their chins
smoothed it?
and I remember lanolin
and think how the farm is being rounded
gentled like pebbles by the leisurely insistence of water
she started to leak
but instead of fixing it
we just put in that old bathtub.
That
he has a way of emphasizing
did the job.

I can see George the pragmatist who adapts
and steps briskly past problems
and marches us over
to the old farmhouse
with its fallen floors
and its dusting of ghosts.
John is Nervous Nelly
but George barges in
as he did the day
he carried Irene over the threshold of their new life:
it was logs in and out
but we brought in the water
and electricity
plastered the walls
and it did us just fine
'til Mom had her stroke
and the big house was too big
for her to keep
so she and Dad
switched with us.
I barely have time to follow
glance at the history all fallen in
before he gently ushers me out
and slams the door.
George lives in the present;
farmers have to have dry eyes.

Back in the yard
he shows me his vehicles.
In the Depression
Dad'd come back

from the CNE
with ribbons and candy
and four hundred dollars;
that'd buy fifty acres of land.
The man who bricked this house earned only
ninety cents a day
and I've got a hundred thousand
tied up in that car and truck!
Grandpa'd roll over in his grave.

Here he stops
sweeps his eyes
over all he's shown:
Just a bit of small talk, but
I'll never sell this farm.
I don't know what he and his sister will do
gestures at son John
lost in words
and waves west where his daughter
has settled in the States
but I'll have nothing
to do with the losing of
this land.

That lost shoe

Every night for her first year here, she dreamt of fire, woke to the phantom smoke and sirens, the roil of soaked bed sheets, the chest so coffin-tight it squeezed fear from her eyes in fat drops. No wonder. She was born in the middle of an Aberdeen air raid, her auntie coaxing her into a world that she didn't want to enter, waves of ungainly Junkers and Focke-Wulfs lumbering in off the Channel and Messerschmitts snarling and darting madly amid the *CRUMP* of anti-aircraft fire and the world going mad all about her slippery ingress.

She remembers still the warnings howled at night, the rousings from deep sleep into surge, a nightdress running across dew-damp lawns, the shelters cramped with crouching and the smell of sweat and cringing every time the earth trembled, the heebie-jeebies dancing like fireflies wild above them.

She remembers her mother hanging laundry on the long line so summer could work its soothing, and then the shadowstorm of metal and menace swinging in from the east and the search for the lowest spot, the face between the knees, the hands over the head, the ears unwilling to hear the awful words being flung. The re-surfacing to find the clothes shot full of holes, and her wonder at the hatred of someone who would shoot shirts and bloomers, who would rend the trousers of her little brother, the vest of her father, the shawl of her granny. Impassioned eyes boring into the intimacies of their lives, the things they wore close.

She remembers that pair of shoes sent to her by her aunt, black patent leather with a little strap worn across her good white socks, of being in the middle of putting them on one Sunday when the sky began to tumble, and of pelting down the road in her good frock, the one shoe spinning off on its own like a willful child and she couldn't even look back, the way she was being tugged, her sockfoot trying to keep up with the other, everything now unbalanced , soft hard soft hard, the sense of unbearable loss later when, though friends and neighbours looked, there was no longer that left shoe, as if it had been sucked up into the whirling firmament.

And now she herself is getting on in years, fretting over all that has been, and her old auntie, the one who eased her into all that tumult, the one who brusquely wiped the caul from her eyes and set her caterwauling onto the arms and the soft milky breasts of her mother, is coming to visit. And what Anne wants her to do is hold her the way she held her in those first fiery moments, like the firm and welcoming earth, and tell her to hush, the machines of war are silenced over Aberdeen, there is no need to wake and worry, tell her that lost shoes are just that, lost, and looking in vain is a cloud that you yourself pull across the sun.

Where does it go?

When his wife died he was eighty something, the fever was waning that had hyper-heated him all his life, made him a gypsy prospector panning the empty reaches of the world for a glint of an answer, so her grandfather moved back in with his daughter and grandchildren, taught the *bambinos* Italian, bounced them on his knees on Saturday afternoons while the Metropolitan Opera poured pure and brave from the big console radio, and he translated with his gnarled and rock-rough hands, drawing music for them in the sunlit parlour.

He let them play with the nuggets that he carelessly kept in Aspirin bottles, the gold bewitched them with its liquid luster, its wanderlust solidified, it must be millions they dreamed as they rolled the gleaming pebbles, as they imagined the Territories empty of all but the old man and his desire, singing arias to the bears and the rushing streams.

Where did that gold go? What happened to the rich foreign words like *coloratura* that he dropped into their eagerness like an old bird feeding its last batch of open-mouthed young? Who has that broad scratched pan that sluiced gravel from the Nahanni and the Mackenzie? How do things once so heavy in your palms evaporate just like that?

My own grandfather was a dentist, and when the drill was not whining, when the chair was not filled with pain and spittle and twisting legs and he sat absorbed in his lab by the smiles he was building for the toothless, he let me play with the precious mercury he mixed into amalgams to fill the gaps where excess and neglect had eaten away what once was.

Mercury, a whisper. Liquid. But not wet, never wet, it rolled in my hands like silver-white dry teardrops, moulding themselves into the lifelines, filling the riverbeds of my future. Slowly diminished, as the afternoon radio shows, baseball mostly, came and went, until none remained to catch the light. I'd ask, he'd put down the dentures, the cigarette that was little more than ash and a roil of smoke, he'd pour me more into the begging bowl of my hand.

Where did my grandfather go the late day he lay down to rest his eyes before supper, and never again awoke? What happened to his gleaming instruments, the mahogany cabinets with the frosted glass doors? Where did the mercury go, and go again, as I heedlessly sluiced it and listened to fly balls drop into grassy outfields in far places like Los Angeles? When did radio drift into static? The answer is elemental. Things must go. Deep. Into our fertile and fragile minds, into these frail and pretty bodies that, all too soon, like evening coming on, themselves go back to the solid and certain soil.

Joe Sherman and I are discussing razors

The newly shorn Joe Sherman
savouring the air on a now smooth face
and rubbing his hand across close-cropped head
is feeling vaguely anonymous
even reborn.

We begin a discussion on the relative merits of razors
two monks moving into the Zen of steel and Teflon.
We agree that electric, which we both used as young men
now buzzes like a gossipmonger's noise
and burns our skin. He tells me he kept his father's
used it long after his dad died, then abandoned it
to where it now sits like a tiny unplugged totem on his dresser.
I tell him I used my dad's triple floating head Philishave
the day of his funeral, a gesture of solidarity
but later tossed it as part of a purge when my mother died.

He's been using a twin-blade
but Joe's excited about the new Quattro.
We grin, repeat the word together
Quattro
rolling our tongues as if around fine wine
Quattro
Quattro
we are the Quattro Choir, we are the singers of skimmed skin
the questers who wonder:
will the fourth blade be the optimum?
will there one day be an eight-edged head?
is there a law of diminishing returns for razor blades?

is there ever such thing as the perfect shave?

We sip our cooling coffees
in the Charlottetown Market
morning movement
two middle-aged men becoming their fathers
while micron by micron, mantra by mantra
the day stubbles on into that neverending shadow.

A train

A train is a long lie you keep telling yourself
you tell yourself you tell yourself you tell yourself you tell yourself
you are a dharma bum and between you and there is all open, all air.

You didn't think, so stunned was your brain by the late-day sun as you
sprawled on the steep grass of the railway cut, you didn't think, when
you saw the train slow, and hesitate, you just impulsed, free-wheeled
it down the embankment onto the clinkers and scrambled up into the
empty open car, the whim upon you, a cloak of invisibility. You felt
your heart lurch with the first tentative tug of the engine, felt the fear
give way to fervour, you lay back in the rush, seeing nothing of your
leave-taking except clouds disentangling themselves from tenacious
tree-tops.

Distance grew, day diminished, the route blurring by in a montage
of ticks and clacks and rattles, of barns with milkings yawning on, of
headlight highways shivering like thin-threaded necklaces, of a steel
river sewing together backyards with faces being taffy-pulled, then
further flattened like the pennies you lay on tracks, the day distorted
by the wind in your head and the supperless belly stretching you thin
and the last pitiless rays of the sun leaving you bereft so you must curl
in a corner and hug yourself into uneasy sleep.

Awoke
to the utter stillness of dawn and tall trees somewhere in the Altered
States of America, as you slept you crossed that line, and now, stiff and
sore you clambered down to the relief of a thundering steaming piss,
Canadian water drilled into thirsty America, and were happy for just
that mindless moment with your dick in your hand and the journey

draining. Until two State Troopers loomed over you with your no ID, no money, no excuses, no destination, took one look at the sad-sack Kerouac, the minstrel in black-face all sooty and teary, took pity and put their guns away, let you phone the father who'd been pacing the night. Your dad picked you up at the border, shook his head and smiled, held you a moment and took you to a breakfast you could not stop consuming, those pancakes floating in maple syrup, and coffee so hot it burned your tongue to sorrow. Then he drove you home up that long dozing highway.

Though you were happy to be back, you'd crossed some frontier that cannot be re-crossed so easily, you'd learned writing outside the margins, now knew the words to the refugee hymn. Those easy streets. Those houses. The people in them. Dinner at the same time every day. Mouths moving monotonously. The road was growing in you, a happy cancer. No cure no cure no cure no cure.

Nearly there

You say *Stop Stop Stop we're nearly there,* the town and the time where you grew up. I am negotiating the winding river road on its outskirts, being careful, as age has taught me, but I obey the urgency in your voice, I pull over.

See that cottage with the green roof, nestled among the spruces, on the other side of the lake, there where the river enters? That's where I almost got my first blow-job. I begin to laugh, reply with something blunt, but sense halts me, there is nothing coarse in your voice, only a yearning, a gentle seeking something out, the way that river is looking for that lake. *My parents were at church, and she came over, we had been friends for years, and she came over, and we were on my bed, laughing and tickling, then somehow kissing, then we found ourselves searching deeper, we found ourselves outside time, we found ourselves without clothes, reverse children of Eden, and that Sunday morning was a garden, rain on the big conifers, making them heavy, dreamy, that evergreen smell and ripples of loonvoice on the otherwise still lake and all the windows open. She leaned over me, her smile changing to something else, her hair, you know she had hair down to her waist, her hair falling over me, tenting me, enveloping me, her eyes opening, and she asked me, "Do you want me to.....you know....?" and her lips parted as if to inhale and her tongue tip flicked out and touched my begging penis so I could barely find my voice enough to whisper a "Yes" so weak I thought the rain would drown my answer. Her gaze held mine, then, more slowly than Sunday falling, she began to lower her head toward my need. Imagine our different desperation then as, at that very apex, we heard the crunch of car wheels at the head of the gravel laneway, my parents, time re-asserting itself, and everything became a stumble, a clumsy falling over ourselves in search of clothes tossed heedless of retrieval. And I'm sure that when my parents entered the cottage to find us faking Scrabble, making up words for what hadn't happened, they could hear our dishevelled hearts beating like those of game birds who have just escaped the snare.*

I re-start the car, slide back out on pavement, rejoin movement, then the houses and stores and cross-streets coalesce into the town growing around you. You speak of who lived here, there, what that was, we look at what it's become. *Look,* so I slow, stop, silence the motor. I must give in to your imperative. There will be more of this starting and stopping, the way one walks through a graveyard, questioning, "Did I know him?" *See that house?* And I see you there, still the trembling virgin, but the girl has changed, she is not nearly so shy, and it is evening and much colder, I can smell woodsmoke . It is Sunday, after supper . *I couldn't believe it. How had I, that pimply awkward boy, ended up making out on her back porch with one of the most popular girls in the school? She had her tongue in my mouth. She took my hand from her hip and guided it up under her skirt into a valley wet and fertile, the meeting of the Tigress and the Euphrates. She said, "I'll let you do it to me, here, now." I didn't know, could you do it standing up? Now was no time to hesitate, so I pulled her to me, wanting so badly to disappear into her, pressed my pelvis against her. Then looked over her shoulder through the window into the black and white of the living room, saw her parents, just ten feet from us, oblivious to their daughter's bare backside, absorbed in their world, saw what they saw, Topo Gigo, the little Italian mouse, a furry boutonniere in a man's pocket imploring the stoic Ed Sullivan to lean down and "Keees me gooodnight, Eddy." And Ed did, without a trace of love, then he turned to the audience and with his outstretched arm and hand, thumb up, brought out a man in a tux who began to balance plates, five of them, spinning on the tips of long long poles, while he unicycled and while the earth lurched, and this girl's parents leaned on their couch to stay in place, he spun those plates, can anyone really do so many things at once? She leaned up to me, wondering, expecting me to meet her steaming mouth, expecting me to slide that long long pole into her, lift her and*

balance her there in that whirling moment. But how could I, with naive little
Topo Gigo just a kiss distant and Ed Sullivan, stern, arms crossed, scowling,
how could I with her parents just feet away, trusting, in the flicker of Sunday
night light? So I shrugged myself together, mumbling, "Sorry, I can't," left
her there rebuffed, bewildered, while the last leaves clattered down like dinner
plates from tired trees.

Streets away, now we're walking. *This was my old house.* I try to see you
there, forty-five years ago, your mother and father the age we are now,
these maples that tower, just newly planted, everything less shaded
then. *My room was up there, and because I was up so high in a house on a*
hill, I had omnivision. One hot summer, when I was sick, confined, I recorded
the world, I watched day and night out that window. That summer I began
to see as I had never seen. I began to notice the tv repair guy, a red-haired
man who lived just there, in the red house, the one that shimmers at sunrise
and sunset, leave for work at 9, come home at 12 for lunch, leave again at
1. I wrote these routines down in a scribbler left over from Social Studies. I
began to notice that every day at 1:10, the barber who lived and cut hair in
the adjacent blue house, put up a CLOSED sign and scuttled next door. At
first I thought, "Mrs. Repairman must be generous, the barber's wife is dead,
she must make him lunch every day, but the house is small, there is no room
at the table for three, so they partake in shifts." We laugh at your simple
world, your omnivision. *I thought all that until the day I saw the door open*
upon Mrs. Repairman in only her bra and panties, a scalding white against
her suntanned skin, a cigarette dangling from her long fingers, a glass of
something golden and ancient in her other hand. And the widowed barber
inclined into her lips, which were plumped in a colour my Catholic mother
called "harlot red." My pencil snapped as I tried to write it down, and my
fingers shook too hard to re-sharpen it. I thought all that until a week later,
the tv repairman burst out of his door early, pulled a hunting rifle from his
repair truck, strode to the blue house roaring, "Come out, you sonofabitch

homewrecker , you don't have a woman so you take mine." But the barbershop
door stayed closed as dead eyes so he stepped back and aimed up at the roof
and started shooting, stopped to reload, kept shooting, until finally he hit the
antenna mast, and the tv antenna slumped slowly onto the roof, like a spent
lover sagging onto the receptacle of his desire, like a storyteller who has drawn
too deeply on recollections collapsing onto his history. The next day the tv
repair family loaded up the truck and moved. The barber kept cutting hair, but
the antenna stayed broken. I guess he quit watching tv. I know I quit looking
out the window.

We are quieter now, we glide along many streets with few words from
you. But then, in a very old part of town, where the sidewalks heave
and names are written into their cement, you reach across and touch
my arm, point to a big place fallen into disrepair. *I loved a girl who lived*
in that house. She had an identical twin, a jabberer, but I loved the shy one,
the hidden one. We'd walk for hours holding hands, never speaking, listening
to the night breathing, under these big trees, under moons both waxing and
waning, under the spell of silence. When we did talk we never spoke of future
or past, of dreams or disappointments, only of the handheld moment. We
inhaled it and repressed our breath. Then her dad was transferred to Toronto.
The day of their move, between Christmas and New Year's, I went over to
say farewell, but I lingered along the way, kicking at snow, not wanting her
to end, so I was late, came around that corner just in time to see the big van
disappear and to see her disappear into the car. I yelled, started to run, but
kept slipping, I had no traction and the winter swallowed my words. I saw her
glove fall from her pocket, saw her white hand reach out, pull the door to her,
then they left. I flailed up to the bare space where they'd been parked, in that
held moment when I'd stood staring at the corner they'd turned, the snow had
begun to cover the pavement. I knelt in the snow, picked up that glove, it was
kid leather, skin soft, still warm from her hand inside. I pressed her heat to my
cold cheek. I kept that glove, intending to mail it to her, knowing I wouldn't,

but pretending, thinking maybe she'd write back, "Thank you, thank you,
come and see me, I so miss you, I want to be with you. Forever." And we'd run
away, not tell our disapproving parents, we wouldn't be too young to elope.
Then one evening I came home from school, to my mother's tears. A phone call
from Toronto, long distance, a faint voice, a car, she and her sister out walking,
a careless car took the shy one, didn't touch the twin, who since then hadn't
said a word. I still have that glove. Somewhere. Once every few years I'll come
across it, pick it up, hold it to my lips, breathe, as if by breathing in and back
out what's left of her, I can re-make her, she'll gaze lovingly at me, we'll know
what we must do to suspend time.

You cease talking, stay stopped, like the remaining half-sister. We
leave what's left of the town in what's left of the light. We will forego
the winding roads that brought us, we will seek the expressway, less
circuitous, less painful, use it. Fast. Faster. It'll take us quickly where
we should be headed: now.